Making Friends—Keeping Friends

Compiled from Teenage Magazine

Group

Loveland, CO

Making Friends—Keeping Friends

Copyright © 1989 by Thom Schultz Publications, Inc.

First Printing

Credits
Edited by Michael D. Warden
Designed by Judy Atwood Bienick
Cover photo by David Priest

Scripture quotations are from the Holy Bible, New International Version. Copyright © 1973, 1978, 1984 International Bible Society. Used by permission of Zondervan Bible Publishers.

Library of Congress Cataloging-in-Publication Data
Making friends—keeping friends / compiled from Teenage magazine

      p.   cm.
   ISBN 0-931529-89-1
     1. Friendship in adolescence. 2. Youth—Religious life.
 I. Teenage magazine (Loveland, Colo.)
  BF724.3.F64M35 1989   89-32326
  158'.25—dc20   CIP

ISBN 0-931529-89-1
Printed in the United States of America

Contents

Section One—**Hand to Hand: Making Friends**

Section Two—Heart to Heart: Keeping Friends

Introduction
Friend to Friend

Dear friend,

I once heard a wise man say, "There are two needs that everyone has in common. One is the need to be loved by others. The other is the need to love."

I have since realized that those two needs are the whole reason we have friends at all. Everyone has these needs you know. I have them; you have them. And they affect the way we relate to others.

We are nice to people we like so they'll like us back. We get angry when someone doesn't act loving toward us. We hang around people our friends will approve of so they won't stop liking us. And we avoid groups that don't appeal to those we want to impress.

Knowing about these needs has helped me understand why my friends are so important to me; why I can't just blow them off even when I really want to. I know now why it's so easy to be hurt and to hurt others. It's because all it takes is a word to cut into a friend's heart. You can really hurt someone who hurts you if you want.

I've learned.

During my sophomore year in high school, my best friend, Trey, started dating this beautiful girl named Barbara. As their relationship got more serious I saw Trey less and less. I became jealous of his time, and I was hurt at his insensitivity to our friendship.

Although I never said anything to him, I quietly began to comment to our other friends about his rude betrayal of our friendship, and how shallow and self-centered he was. It wasn't until a few years later that I learned how deeply hurt he was when he heard what I had said. My opinion mattered to him, and I abused the trust he had placed in me.

I also know about all the games we friends play with each other. I know how to play the popularity game. I know how to exclude people without being really rude, and how it feels to go with the crowd—even when I know it's wrong. You've probably learned how to hide your feelings, like I have, and put on a face that you think your friends will like better than the real you.

If you've played these games for a while then you already know the catch.

You never win.

As I kept playing the games, I realized that it really wasn't me they liked. It was this face I had put on. My friends didn't understand *me*—the me deep inside. They understood the fun me, the outgoing me, the fake me. It was all like a part in a play. It was all a game.

Have you ever felt that way? I'll tell you, at first I didn't know what to do. But eventually I found the truth. I discovered the secret to being real, to being accepted, to having true friends.

Love.

That's what this book is all about. The art of loving and being loved. It's about how to stand up for what you believe without losing those you care about. It's about working through problems with others, and winning them over rather than cutting them down.

It's about meeting needs. That's love in action! Jesus knew that secret. The whole reason he came to Earth was to meet our need. He gave us what nobody else could give—his own life. And in that gift we discover how to love. "We love, because he first loved us." The simple rule is: Love creates love. When we take our eyes off ourselves and really try to meet others' needs, our own needs are met, almost automatically. I'm still not sure how it works. But it does.

So now when I'm with my friends I ask myself, "What is the most loving thing I can do for this person?" Sometimes the answer has been to buy them lunch that week or to send them a card just to say how I appreciate them. Sometimes when my friends and I have gone through a rough time, the most loving thing I can do is to give them space. But whatever it is, I try to do it. And somehow through it all, I am filled with love—Jesus' love.

So as you read these pages, train yourself to

think about meeting others' needs rather than having your own needs met. And let Jesus speak to you. He's there on every page. And he's with you, right in the big thick of every relationship you have. Pay attention to what he tells you. You know his advice is sound. And besides, he is the best friend you'll ever have.

Or ever need.

The Lord bless you,
A friend

Section One

Hand to Hand: Making Friends

Chapter 1
Making Friends

You look great today!

Have you ever met someone who somehow had the power to make you feel good about yourself, about the world, about life? What I mean is a person who consistently offered you a refreshing comment or kind word. Someone with that certain brightness and touch that left you feeling smart, spirited, even jubilant.

Someone like Dave Bryant. Dave was a classmate of mine in high school. Being close friends, he and I weathered many storms as well as climbed several mountaintops together. But it was the way he listened that fortified me. Others might change the subject, chatter about the latest football game or slip away in boredom. Not Dave.

He'd ask questions, squint and rub his chin as though my thoughts were important. He'd suggest that we sit on a problem for a while, then drop me a note in class or call me the same evening with some new insights he'd discovered about the situation.

Often he'd take my problems more seriously

Making Friends Pretest: What's Your Friendship IQ?

Aristotle said the ideal friendship is one soul in two bodies. Jesus said the greatest love of all is laying down one's life for a friend.

What about your friends? Do you choose friends who mirror your personality and values? Why do you form friendships?

Before you dig into this book, take the following quiz to see where you rank on the friendship scale.

True or False

_____ 1. Teenagers tend to choose friends who are similar to themselves, and friends become more similar as time goes on.

_____ 2. Guys and girls enjoy friendships in different ways and for different reasons. Therefore, girls shouldn't try to be close friends with guys (and vice versa) because it's too confusing.

_____ 3. Friendships have nothing to do with your decision about drug use.

_____ 4. Peer pressure doesn't enter into a real friendship.

_____ 5. The number of friends you have is not very important.

_____ 6. People who have trouble fitting in with others almost always have low social skills.

_____ 7. A real Christian never feels hatred toward anyone.

_____ 8. The most important quality in a friendship is the ability to make others laugh.

continued

_____ 9. After a fight with a friend, the best thing to do is talk it out as soon as possible.

_____10. People who lie to their parents probably aren't trustworthy with others either.

_____11. People who come to your youth group meetings one time, but never come back again, probably just didn't like your group.

_____12. You should never joke with minorities about their ethnicity.

_____13. One of the most meaningful things you can do to let someone know you like them is just to listen to them.

_____14. Criticism is okay, as long as it's really deserved.

_____15. As long as your non-Christian friends can watch the way you live, it isn't necessary to talk to them about your faith.

Briefly check your answers. Then, after you've read through the book, come back and take this test again. You may be surprised by how much you've learned.

Now read on!

Answers

1. True (Chapter 5).
2. False (Chapter 9).
3. False (Chapter 4).
4. False (Chapter 10).
5. True (Chapter 4).
6. False (Chapter 7).
7. False (Chapter 13).
8. False (Chapter 1).
9. True (Chapter 11).
10. True (Chapter 2).
11. False (Chapter 3).
12. False (Chapter 6).
13. True (Chapter 8).
14. False (Chapter 12).
15. False (Chapter 14).

Joan Anderson

than I would. His favorite expression was "I'm in this with you." He had that magic capability to identify with me whether I was high, low or in-between. He never failed to re-ignite me when my life looked like a rain out.

Admittedly, I haven't known many Daves in my life. But there could be more like him—many more. In fact, you could be one. Do you think you'd like to be a person who lights people up rather than snuffs them out? If so, read on.

► What's the Secret?

Basically, Dave was an encourager. He knew how to build up people with words and actions in just the right way at just the right moment. He encouraged others like me because he *cared* about people. If he had encouraged just to get a good reaction or to get in good with someone, that would have been crass manipulation. I have seen myself try to do this with people by "buttering them up." But this wasn't Dave's motive at all. He genuinely loved the people he was building up. Concern, care and love are the prerequisites for true encouragement. With that in mind, let me suggest four methods you can use to light up people's lives, to make friends.

► Four Ways to Light up Lives

1. Be a captive audience and learn to applaud those around you. Someone has said people's greatest craving is simply to be appreciated. Jesus knew this well. Not only did he teach, but he also listened. He was a "captive audience" to all who came to him with a need. He never rushed anyone or turned them away. After listening, he often responded with gentle applause, that is, a compliment or a bit of personal praise.

A Japanese proverb states, "One kind word can warm three winter months." And Mark Twain said, "I can live a whole week on one good compliment." Think about that. The last time someone let you know something about you that they appreciated, how did you feel? You probably straightened up, walked a little taller and felt a little happier.

Suppose you began making it a habit to applaud all your friends, acquaintances and relatives for their good points and deeds. You'd probably become quite a popular person, if you did it sincerely and honestly.

How do you do it? Just keep your eyes open. Tell people one good thing about the way they look. Take note of something kind or insightful that they said or did and express your appreciation. Let them know how you enjoyed an article in the school paper. Or their fine performance in a game. Or their hard work on a project. Whenever you see something you like, tell the one who did it about it. Before long, people will be beating a path to your mouth. You will have become an encourager.

2. Openly express your love to those you care for. One woman I heard about was feeling great despair that her husband no longer loved her. He just never said "I love you." The counselor she was seeing met with the husband and asked him about this. He replied: "The day I married her 25 years ago I told her I loved her. If the situation changes, I'll let her know." That's a tragedy because all of us need assurance and reinforcement. This can be done through kind deeds. But it is most simply expressed through three words—"I love you."

I remember once in seminary while I was hospitalized with acute depression, a friend came by every week to visit me. One week he brought a small Mattel truck to put on my shelf. He told me that whenever I was down to imagine that he and I were driving in it together, praying and joking. He told me, "I want you to know that I'm going to stick with you till this is over. I love you, buddy." When he told me that, he lit up my life. We all need that affirmation, that expression of honest love.

3. Remind others of people who nearly failed but triumphed in the end. This is especially important to those on the verge of giving up—on algebra, a girlfriend or even life itself. The scriptures are filled with examples. Consider Romans 15:4. "For everything that was written in the past was written to teach us, so that through endurance and the encouragement of the scriptures we might have hope." God's Word is meant to build us up, not rip us apart. How does it work?

I recently read a story about a fireman trying to rescue a child from a burning building. He had climbed a ladder past several stories, but above him the flames suddenly broke from a window and licked out at him fiercely. He faltered and backed down the ladder immediately.

Frank, the frantic friendship chaser

Someone in the crowd below noted his fear and began shouting, "Give him a cheer." The crowd yelled, "You can do it. Go on up! You can make it!" The fireman was encouraged and rescued the child.

That's what the scriptures are like. When people believe they can't do it, we can show them the story of David or Elijah or Mary or Ruth, all of whom faltered and wanted to give up at certain points in their lives. From those scriptures people are crying out: "You can do it. Look at me—by God's grace I made it. So can you. Don't give up. We're right behind you."

That's true encouragement. By using those stories as well as those from your own experience, you will challenge others to keep going when things get tough.

4. Talk about our future as Christians. More than any other person on Earth, a Christian has reason to hope. Hope of being made perfect, dwelling in heaven and knowing Jesus face to face. Our future hope as Christians is a primary theme in scripture. A large percentage of the Bible is concerned with our future. Why is this? As Paul says, so that we might "encourage one another and build each other up" (1 Thessalonians 5:11).

Once while working in New Jersey, a close friend of mine came by to talk. She was experiencing fear and frustration and feeling like it was all over between her and Christ. We began discussing the power of God, his love and his goals for our lives. We talked especially of heaven and what it'd be like. As we shared, I noted that she began to perk up. When the evening was over, she remarked, "This was fun. I feel like a new person already."

All we chatted about were the facts of scripture and our hope as Christians. But those truths have a way of rekindling faith and hope in human hearts.

► It's Your Choice

So, do you want to be a people-builder or a people-breaker? It's really not difficult to build people up. Simply listen to and applaud others through honest praise. Express personal love and support. Remind others of people who won over big problems. And talk about our future as Christians. Draw upon God's love inside you to care for others. And, ultimately, you'll become a candle God can use to light up others' lives.

Mark Littleton

Chapter 2
Learning to Lean

Any friend will tell you that trust is one of the most important qualities of a strong friendship. So in order to make new friends and strengthen old friendships, you have to learn to be trustworthy. That means respecting those things your friends hold as valuable, and letting them see the real you. Until you do, they can never learn to trust you or to love you for who you really are.

Here's a little test to measure your trust factor. Before you go through the questions, decide how trusting you think you are (super-trusting, medium-trusting or anti-trusting). Now go through the test, and see how well you graded yourself.

DIRECTIONS: Place an "X" on the trust scale that best answers each question.

When a friend reveals personal information, do you immediately tell others what your friend just told you?

When a friend shares personal information, assume that what's said is meant for you alone.

In trust, Brian told Jill he thought his dad had a job offer. It meant their family might be moving across the country. But Brian's dad didn't get the job, and for weeks Brian battled the rumor of his move. Understandably, Brian was hurt that Jill had shared what he considered a secret.

If people want others to know about themselves, they will take the responsibility of telling. If you feel a strong need to relay information, ask permission from the source.

Do you find yourself complaining and saying negative things about others?

Constantly casting a dark shadow on conversations reflects what kind of person you are. Most often people will trust those they know who "put the best construction" on everything. If you're a person who has the reputation of forgiving, listening and offering the benefit of the doubt, you'll be like a magnet. Those positive qualities will attract others to share themselves with you.

In conversations, do you stretch the facts to make stories juicier and more exciting?

If a friend says, "Mike is *so* cute," do you send Cupid-like rumblings saying your friend really likes Mike and wants to go out with him? It won't be long before the word is out: You're someone who blows things out of proportion. Before people confide in you again, they will hesitate because you might exaggerate whatever they say.

Do you jump to conclusions without carefully listening?

Assumptions can get you into trouble. Feelings can be easily misunderstood. Restate and check what you're hearing. Don't be afraid to ask your friend what you think she's just said. Simply ask, "Do I hear you saying . . . ?" and she can correct you if you're wrong. Accurate communication is crucial for building trust.

When talking with friends, do you often whisper and exclude others from your conversations?

If your friendly lunchroom conversations turn to touchy subjects, learn to reserve them for more private settings. Shifty glances and hushed voices signal mistrust. Others begin thinking: "Maybe they're talking about me. I wonder why?

What did I do to make them talk about me?"
Even though they might be mistaken, it's easy for
others to jump to unhealthy conclusions about
you and your trust if you act that way.

When coming home late, do you sneak around and cover up your whereabouts?

Parents will treat you more like an adult when
you build trust with them. Two or three times of
your parents' discovering who you *really* were
with and where you *really* were will shatter the
delicate foundation of parental trust.

Darlene learned the hard way. She started hanging around a group of friends who were into
drinking and partying. Darlene knew her parents
wouldn't let her go to Friday night's party, so she
told them she was doing something else. Later
her parents found out she'd lied. Their trust level
sank.

Be honest with your mom and dad. They'll appreciate and celebrate your maturity. If you feel
like you must be secretive at home, ask yourself
why. Re-evaluate your behavior and be honest
with yourself. Are you secretive because you're
doing hurtful things? Let your sneakiness be a
signal for potential personal change.

When asked about certain things, do you fib and tell little white lies?

People grow in trust when they learn that you're honest and not afraid of risking the truth. But lies have a way of haunting you. When people discover contradictions and falsehoods, they see that you can't be trusted. Practice being honest, straightforward and open.

When you're with someone, do you think he or she mistrusts you?

Making assumptions about mistrust breeds mistrust. If you wonder about and question people's motives for friendship, you sow the seeds of mistrust.

Friends *will* trust you if you truly love and care for them. Because of your love, they'll know you always want the best for them and never want to hurt them unnecessarily.

Trust grows out of love. Relationships bound in love automatically create trust as a byproduct.

Do you find it difficult to care about friends who confide in you?

Believe in your friends. Accept the fact that they're confiding in you. The more you feel that your friends trust you to keep their secrets, the

A Word About Friends

The word "friend" appears 52 times in the Bible; the word "friends" appears 49 times. Here are some "friendly" Bible verses to read for more thoughts on friendship:

Ecclesiastes 4:9-12 —Friends stand by each
other.

Matthew 7:12 —Treat friends like you
want to be treated.

Luke 6:30-31
—Friends give without
conditions.

John 13:34 —Friends are known by
their love for each
other.

Romans 12:10 —Friends honor each
other.

Romans 14:19 —Friends encourage, not
discourage.

Romans 15:1-3, 7 —Friends support others,
even in bad times.

Galatians 6:2 —Friends lean on one
another.

Philippians 2:3-4 —Friends meet others'
needs before their own.

Colossians 4:6 —Friends think about
what they say to others.

1 Thessalonians 5:11—Friends strengthen
each other.

Hebrews 13:1-3, 16 —Friends care for the
friendless.

1 Peter 1:22 —Friends love deeply.

1 Peter 4:8 —Friends forgive each
other.

more you'll do just that! Knowing they're counting on you helps you be a more faithful friend.

Now count your "None of the Time" Choices.

TOTAL:

If you have all (or almost all) marked in this range, congratulations! Keep up the good work! You're a trusted friend and someone people will seek out.

Count your "Some of the Time" Choices.

TOTAL:

If most of your marks are in this range, reread the questions. Think about some of the times you said and did these things. Is there a pattern to these situations or are they isolated instances? Work at changing any caution areas in your life.

Count your "All of the Time" Choices.

TOTAL:

Warning! If all (or almost all) of your marks are in this range, you may discover your friends abandoning you because they can't trust you. Carefully work on these behaviors. Be aware of your actions and pray for God's special help in building trustworthy relationships.

Joani Schultz

Chapter 3
Fitting In

How Friendly Are You?

How welcome do you make others feel? Before you read this chapter, take a minute to check out your friendliness factors. Respond to each statement below as honestly as you can by placing a checkmark in the box that best describes you.

Friendly or Not?

	Always	Often	Sometimes	Never
1. I'm at ease with people my own age, even when they're strangers.	☐	☐	☐	☐
2. I'm at ease with older people.	☐	☐	☐	☐
3. I'm courteous to adults.	☐	☐	☐	☐
4. I appear cheerful rather than sulky.	☐	☐	☐	☐
5. I'm equally comfortable in the company of one or more people.	☐	☐	☐	☐

continued

	Always	Often	Sometimes	Never
6. I go out of my way to make newcomers or strangers feel welcome.	□	□	□	□
7. I read newspapers and listen to news programs regularly.	□	□	□	□
8. I have an interesting hobby that I can talk about.	□	□	□	□
9. I try to find out what others are interested in and then talk about that.	□	□	□	□
10. I entertain my friends *without* relying on television.	□	□	□	□
11. I pay attention to people who don't readily interest me.	□	□	□	□
12. I look at the person who's speaking to me.	□	□	□	□
13. I wait for someone to finish talking before I speak.	□	□	□	□

Now, count the checkmarks in each column. If your largest total is in the "always" column, you're very friendly; the "often" column, you're average, but you should work on being more friendly; the "sometimes"

continued

column, there's lots of room to improve; the "never" column, it's time to take a serious look at yourself.

Do you find it difficult to be friendly? Stop and think for a minute about the balance between effort and result. Attention to a few friendly habits is a small price to pay for having good friends.

This chapter gives some sound advice for helping other people feel comfortable around you. And the advice is equally valuable if you are the one who feels left out. The sooner you begin to include others in your life, the sooner you'll find friends who really appreciate you.

Neoma Foreman

Robbie edged his way toward the youth room. He hesitated. *"I don't know what I'm doing here,"* he thought as a few "regular" youth group members zoomed past him.

Hands in his hip pockets, wearing a self-conscious glance, Robbie scanned the meeting place. It felt as awkward as riding a bike for the first time. He knew he could do it, but that didn't ease the queasy sensation of the dreaded "firsts."

Entering the room, he focused on an old hand-me-down couch overflowing with vaguely familiar kids from school. They were piling on each other's laps, teasing and laughing.

"That does look fun . . . ," Robbie thought. *"So why do I wish I could get out of here?"*

Then Robbie spied the group's leader. She barely managed to break away from what she was doing to say, "Glad you could join us tonight . . . I don't think I know your name."

"Rob (cough) Robbie," he stuttered as if he'd never revealed his true identity before.

"Nice to meet you," she smiled, burying herself in her get-ready details.

"She sounded nice enough," Robbie thought.

The trouble is, later she forgot to introduce him to the group. And when he was leaving, she shouted, "Bye, Richard!"

Robbie never went to another youth meeting. Not that it was so bad, or boring, or that people were mean. It's just that nobody seemed to care if he was there or not.

☐ ☐ ☐

► The Problem

Multiply Robbie's story hundreds of times. Rearrange the circumstances and juggle the names, and you'll begin to understand why some kids never feel a part of a youth group.

Imagine Robbie's feelings and what the youth group's actions said to him. How do you reach out and accept the "Robbies" in your church and school?

It takes work to include people in your life. Making people feel as though they belong creates images of the "love stuff" Jesus talks about. But it isn't easy.

► God's Perspective

God doesn't ask the impossible. You *do* have what it takes to care for others. It's just that sometimes we lose perspective of how God sees us—and how God sees the other people in our lives. When it comes to accepting others, remember these two God-views:

1. God uses you to show his love. Think about what went through Robbie's mind during his only visit to the youth group. Watching kids laugh and goof around on the couch *did* make an impression on him: The church, God's people, have lots of fun. But when no one reached out to Robbie, he felt excluded and unimportant. If the people he could see and touch didn't care, how could an invisible God love him?

You have the exciting responsibility of making God's love visible! Your worth shines through words like, "Now you are the body of Christ, and each one of you is a part of it" (1 Corinthians 12:27). Being Christ's body means that your welcoming smile, helping hands or hugging arms are really the Lord's!

2. Loving each other is loving Jesus. Robbie's experience at youth group was all too typical. The leader who greeted Robbie had good intentions, but didn't follow through. In the meeting's busyness—planning a summer tour, Saturday's carwash and a visit to the nursing home—the group overlooked the closest ministry possible. Robbie was right there beside them—representing Christ.

Just imagine. When you include someone, you're actually welcoming and including Jesus. Christ said, "Whatever you did for one of the least of these brothers of mine, you did for me!" (Matthew 25:40).

So take a closer look at the shy girl in your youth group, the rowdy guy on your bus and the new kid next to you in biology class. They're all people God is using—waiting to be loved.

▶ Ways to Include People in Your Life

Consider these down-to-earth suggestions as you begin the adventure of involving others in your life:

● *Begin your youth group meetings with a "sharing" experience.* Each week, make up incomplete sentences to be answered at the start of each time together. (Examples: "My favorite sport is . . . ," "When I'm alone I like to . . . ," or "Right now I feel . . .") Write them down and place them in a "starter jar." Have each person draw out one "starter" and complete the sentence.

● *Call people by name.* It feels good to have your name remembered. Saying "Hi" is fine, but saying "Hi, Dan" is even better!

● *Take the initiative.* Make it your responsibility to welcome "outsiders." Ask them questions, invite them to join your group, save a place for them to sit beside you in the cafeteria or at church. Let them know their presence makes a difference.

● *Head up a "clique-attack."* Break the exclusion habit by avoiding private "in" jokes—whispering and saying negative things about people not considered "in."

● *Greet each person who is there.* Make an extra effort to acknowledge people's presence.

Fitting in

Even the "old timers" like to feel valued and appreciated.

● *Plan a surprise kidnapping party.* Call and warn a new person's parents of your friends' early plans and arrival. Treat the person to a rousing wake-up song and breakfast at a nearby restaurant.

● *Celebrate special days.* Remember birthdays and plan creative surprises. For example, in your youth group, all the July birthdays could be celebrated one day in July. Or for a different twist, one month celebrate all the people whose names begin with the letter A through D. Each month continue through the alphabet.

● *Create a brother/sister strategy at church.* Match new or inactive people to those who are actively involved in your group. Encourage the active members to get acquainted with the new people. They can inform them of what's happening or provide rides to youth group. They can also be on the lookout during meetings, making certain their "brother" or "sister" is doing okay.

Joani Schultz

Chapter 4

Playing the Popularity Game

Oh, to be popular . . .

You never have to sit alone in the cafeteria. You win the student council election by a landslide. You're picked as head cheerleader—or captain of the football team. You're invited to all the best parties. Walking through the halls, you feel like a star—everyone waves and smiles.

Popularity is a consuming goal in most high schools. We all want to be well-liked. We thirst for the approval, acceptance and love from those around us. Many people feel that the best way to find this kind of love is by taking shortcuts, by playing the popularity game.

But there's a problem with the popularity game. It costs too much. In order to play, you often have to leave your values behind. Becoming one of the Popular People means you must play by *their* rules. You must conform. In my high school, that meant you dated only other Popular People.

And the rule for making out was: *no rules*.

I remember a Christian girl named Sue who was intelligent, churchgoing, good-looking and fun to be around. But she was driven by an intense desire to be popular. So when Steve (one of the Popular People) asked her out, she quickly accepted—even though she really didn't like the guy and knew he had a raunchy reputation.

Several weeks later, Sue discovered she was pregnant. She was miserable, humiliated and alone—a victim of her own compromising quest to be popular.

The popularity game has lots of unwritten rules. Rules about dating, drinking, friends, dress, talk, fun. And many of these rules require a sacrifice of conscience and perhaps of Christian morals. The cost is heavy.

► Popularity Is Temporary

Like most games, the popularity game has a time limit. High school popularity fades quickly after graduation. And all of the invested time, effort and stress to be a part of the Popular People is forever lost.

I know some people who have tried to hang on to the Popular People lifestyle after high school. Three girls on the cheerleading squad at my high school were hard-core Popular People. They dated the football "heroes," attended the "right" parties, won the school elections, and acted very coldly toward the kids who were not part of the Popular People.

Predictably, after high school everyone parted

and began building their adult lives—everyone, that is, except these three girls. They stuck together and tried to continue their exclusive little club. They continued to laugh at the "nerds" who had been their classmates. But the nerds began leaving town and attending colleges or landing good jobs. They probably never knew that the three girls back home were laughing.

Now, after 15 years, I still see these three former cheerleaders. They don't seem to laugh much anymore. Once a week they gather at a local restaurant and sit at the same little table. They seem lonely. Their cold, aloof, "popular" way of treating others has left them with only each other.

► No Time for Self-Development

For many people, the quest for popularity is consuming. So much time is spent on "fitting in" that there's little time left for self-development. Striving to become like the rest of the crowd stifles individuality and creativity.

There was a guy in my class who was certainly not among the Popular People. Matter of fact, he was one they really laughed at and ridiculed. But ol' Ron didn't mind. He was a real individual.

Ron was about the only guy in our school with a crew cut. He carried a briefcase and drove to school in a beat-up old yellow school bus. The popular kids laughed when he took a job as a "skate cop" (supervisor at a skating rink). But Ron loved it. He whizzed around the rink, blowing his whistle and yelling, "Slow down or I'll throw you out!" And the popular kids laughed when Ron went to work part time as a special deputy for the sheriff.

But Ron continued to do the things that interested him.

Today Ron is one of the happiest guys I know. He's a police detective. And those high school years, when he was determined to live out his individuality, became the foundation for his satisfaction now.

We become more like the people God wants us to be when we're not afraid to be ourselves. The Popular People would have us try to be someone we're not.

▶ Stepping on Others

The cost of the popularity game is often paid by those who aren't even on the team. By its very nature, popularity is not for everyone. Unpopular people are necessary so that Popular People can remain an "elite class." Popular People are aware of this principle and perpetuate it by making sure the unpopular stay unpopular.

This manifests itself in such practices as making an unpopular person feel very uncomfortable if he or she chooses to sit at the Popular Table at lunch, or teasing a popular kid for spending time with an unpopular kid. "You went out with Joe Schmitzer? How sick!"

I've known many popular kids who were not among the Popular People. That is, even though popular, they did not play the popularity game. They were not afraid to associate with the unpopular kids. Many of their closest friends were

The popularity game

How to Love the Unlovable

"Christians are supposed to love everybody"—how often have you heard that? But you don't love everybody, and that makes you feel guilty.

You need to realize that you don't naturally relate to everybody positively. But Jesus taught that you must show love to everybody. To love your enemies doesn't mean that you feel affectionate toward them, but that you act in a loving manner toward them.

Why might you have a hard time loving some people? It could be that they've hurt you. Or it could be that they cling to you like a vine to a tree. Or it may just be that their personality mixes with yours like matter with antimatter. Whatever the surface issue might be, the root problem is that you have failed to see in that person what God sees in them—someone worth dying for.

What to Do

You may be able to think of a number of other reasons why you *shouldn't* show love to certain people, but here are some basic guidelines to help you learn to show love even to the most hard-core, hard-to-like people.

1. Think of the last time you were really irritated by someone who is hard-to-love. How did you respond? _____
_____

How do you think Jesus would have responded in that same situation? _____
_____

continued

The next time you're with that "special person," try doing what you think Jesus would do. You may be surprised to see how differently the other person will react.

2. Memorize Matthew 25:40: "The King will reply, 'I tell you the truth, whatever you did for one of the least of these brothers of mine, you did for me.'" Write it on an index card, and tape it in a prominent place inside your locker. Then the next time you're assigned to a lab partner who isn't exactly your first choice, say to yourself, "The Jesus I claim to love is inside them." You will find Jesus strangely waiting to be encountered and loved in even the most obnoxious people.

3. Take some time this week to get to know that quiet guy who sits alone at lunch, and then introduce him to a group of your Christian friends. Encourage your friends to share the responsibility to reach out to the hard-to-love.

4. Try to see hard-to-love people as a challenge, and not a plague. Make an effort to overlook their irritating qualities, and see who they really are. Working toward understanding others is the first step toward really appreciating them.

Begin today the adventure of loving the unlovable.

Tony Campolo

real "nobodies" in the minds of the Popular People. Who your friends are can reveal whether or not you're playing the popularity game.

► Disciples' Popularity Contest

The popularity game is not new. It's been around for a long time. After stepping inside after a long walk, Jesus asked his disciples, "What were you arguing about on the road?" They looked around at each other, feeling a little sheepish. Nobody wanted to answer Jesus, because on the road they had been arguing about who was the greatest.

Jesus knew what was said on the road. He sat down, called the disciples over to him and said, "If anyone wants to be first, he must be the very last, and the servant of all."

What an incredible thing to say! Christ wants the world to turn upside down.

Suppose Jesus would come to your school to pick out the top young people. Who would they be, measured by his standards? Would he choose the Popular People? Some of them might be on Jesus' list, but the vast majority on his list would be nobodies: people who quietly go about loving and caring for others.

After Christ told his disciples that greatness demands that they become servants, he picked up a little kid, and said "Whoever welcomes one of these children in my name welcomes me" (Mark 9:33-37). Jesus was exposing the emptiness of the popularity game. He was telling us that instead of squabbling about popularity, we should be looking for opportunities to serve the nobodies. By serving them, we serve Christ.

Spending time with the nobodies—the nerds, the unpopular people—doesn't fit the popularity game. Matter of fact, the Popular People will probably laugh at you. They may ridicule you and see to it that you never become one of the Popular People.

But you won't be alone. You'll be in good company. For you see, Jesus himself never won the popularity game. If he had, he wouldn't have died on a cross. Jesus wasn't interested in playing games. He had no time for games. He was too busy serving those around him—the lonely, the nerds, the unpopular people.

And he calls us to do the same.

Thom Schultz

Chapter 5
Flicking Your Clique

"I don't click with any clique, so what do I do?"

"Why does everyone want to be in a clique?"

"What's wrong with being in a clique?"

"How do I break up the cliques in my youth group?"

It seems like every church youth group has cliques—those small, exclusive clusters of friends. Clique members are always together and usually keep everyone else out.

What about your youth group? Have cliques

Rate Your Group

For each statement, rate your youth group on a scale of 0 to 10; circle your answers.

- I see cliques in my youth group.

  0   1   2   3   4   5   6   7   8   9   10

  Never   Always

- Cliques have a negative influence in my youth group.

  0   1   2   3   4   5   6   7   8   9   10

  Never   Always

- My youth group lets clique members do everything together.

  0   1   2   3   4   5   6   7   8   9   10

  Never   Always

- After youth group meetings, some kids go home feeling left out.

  0   1   2   3   4   5   6   7   8   9   10

  Never   Always

- I'm against breaking up cliques at youth group meetings.

  0   1   2   3   4   5   6   7   8   9   10

  Never   Always

Now add up your score. Where does your group fall?

  0-12: "Cliques? No problem!"
  13-25: "Okay, but could do better."
  26-37: "Maybe we *do* have a clique problem."
  38-50: "Alert! Clique overload!"

taken over? Do your group meetings resemble a yard that's just been raked: a lot of little clumps scattered throughout the room? Take this "Rate Your Group" test and see how your group rates. Then move on to the multiple-choice exercise to explore your answer to cliques.

► Questions About Cliques

● *Why do people want to belong to cliques?* Everyone wants to be accepted; no one wants to be left out. When a small group of friends "takes you in," you don't have to worry about being alone, especially at large gatherings. Cliques provide comfort, security and identity.

● *So what about outsiders?* The exact opposite. Outsiders feel no acceptance. They feel left out and unwanted, isolated and cut off. They constantly examine themselves and question why they don't fit in. Most of the answers aren't nice: I'm too fat; I'm too shy; I'm clumsy; I'm a nobody.

Outsiders develop poor self-images when cliques reject them. So they search for other cliques that *will* accept them, and they often join them to cover up their hurt. Someone's life can be completely changed by joining the wrong crowd.

● *How do cliques affect a youth group?* A youth group needs to feel togetherness to be successful. If a clique in your youth group clings together at every activity, your group will have a hard time building togetherness. The clique forms its own youth group and becomes separate from the whole group. For the good of the entire group, you need to join in activities that break

Your "Answer" to Cliques

Knowing your youth group's situation isn't enough. How do you deal with cliques? What would your response be to these "cliquish" situations? Circle the letter that best represents how you'd react in each situation.

1. Bill, a friend in the youth group, tells you there are too many cliques at church. You:
   a. shrug your shoulders and say there's nothing you can do.
   b. tell Bill he's just mad because he's not accepted by any of the cliques.
   c. stand up and announce to the youth group that all cliques must break up.
   d. thank Bill for telling you his thoughts and think about them later.
   e. other: _____

2. Sharon, an unattractive youth group member, wants your clique to invite her to join. You:
   a. ignore her.
   b. tell her to get lost.
   c. deny that you're in a clique.
   d. tell her you'll talk it over with your friends and get back to her.
   e. other: _____

continued

3. You really want to be part of a particular clique. You:
   a. drop hints to the clique members.
   b. pray and hope the group will start liking you.
   c. push your way in and start hanging around the clique members.
   d. tell people in the clique they must accept you or break up.
   e. other: _____

4. Tom, your youth group director, talks about cliques at a meeting and says he doesn't want to see them anymore. You:
   a. tell him teenagers have a right to form cliques.
   b. tell him his demands are easier said than done.
   c. immediately tell your friends to break up their clique.
   d. ask Tom to be willing to discuss it more.
   e. other: _____

   Look back over your answers after you read the rest of this article.

Ways to Develop Togetherness

● **Problem-solving tasks.** When your youth group leader gives you tasks that require working side by side with others, work with people you don't usually hang around with. This helps develop trust and builds new bonds.

● **Non-threatening conversations.** At youth group meetings, sit next to someone who's not in your normal group of friends. Ask non-threatening questions, such as "What classes do you have in school?" and "What's your favorite color? Why?" You'll get to know other kids.

● **Small-group Bible studies.** When your youth group leader asks you to break up into smaller groups, don't automatically sit with the same crowd. Go to another group. Encourage lots of discussion. Show other youth group members you care about what they think.

● **Games and crowdbreakers.** When the group plays games such as relay races, don't immediately team up with your friends. Go out of your way to choose people who usually are left out. Then, as you cheer and pull for each other, they'll feel more a part of the group.

● **Leadership roles.** When your youth group leader is looking for volunteers to head up various committees, suggest to your friends that you each volunteer for a different project. Then ask kids who usually aren't leaders to work on your committee with you.

up cliques and encourage clique members to open up and share with other people.

● *What can you do about youth group cliques?* Perhaps you're in a clique. Sure, it's nice to go to youth group and know that your friends will be there and you won't feel alone. But remember: You're a much-needed member of a *youth group*, not just a clique.

If you want to help make your youth group better, work to develop group togetherness. Here are some ways you can take an active role in smashing clique barriers.

► The "Model Clique"

Jesus had a clique of sorts: his disciples. They met by themselves sometimes. But when others were around, anyone who wanted to join was welcome. Jesus accepted anyone. The people who joined him became members of his community.

That's what a church youth group really is— part of the whole body of Christ. Why not make your entire youth group one big, accepting, loving clique—open for anyone to join? Just keep Jesus' example in mind.

Alan Maki

Befriending the Friendless

Use these tips to practice accepting people who are new and different.

● **Put yourself in their shoes.** You were once new and may have some weird traits of your own. How did your self-esteem grow?

● **Overlook their differences.** Don't concentrate on how they look or act differently than other people do. God says, "Man looks at the outward appearance, but the Lord looks at the heart" (1 Samuel 16:7).

● **Don't judge.** Accept others for who they are. But don't compromise your values or personal ethics (Romans 14:1-13).

● **Realize acceptance grows slowly.** Before diving into a pool, it's best to test the water. Give people time to grow comfortable around you. Learn when to talk, what to say and how much.

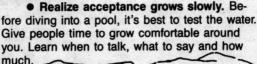

continued

● **Let people be themselves.** Everyone is unique, created in the image of God (Psalm 139). Don't try to shape them in your image.

● **Accept the person as God's gift.** Focus on the Giver, the one who is sovereign, the one who doesn't make mistakes. Even those who are "hard to handle" can help you become a better person.

Everyone wants to belong. We feel secure when we're included. "Accept one another, then, just as Christ accepted you, in order to bring praise to God" (Romans 15:7).

By building up others, we meet their need for self-esteem and bring them to the point where they can say "I am loved."

Breaking down barriers of prejudice

Chapter 6
Tearing Down Social Walls

It's not easy being a banana. A banana isn't just a fruit—it's a slang term used to describe a Japanese-American—someone who has yellow Oriental skin on the outside, but white American culture inside, beneath the peel.

Being a banana bothers me because people look at my black hair and almond eyes and automatically categorize me as a rice eater, chopstick user and Honda driver. But stereotypes don't fit individuals. Though I may look like I've just gotten off the boat from Japan, in reality I was born in Iowa, eat pizza, use a fork and drive a Chevette.

The stares and jokes have been painful, but I've found that even people with World War II "Jap" prejudices have accepted me and loved me—it's just a matter of understanding.

Here's some advice on how to relate to people of other races and ethnic groups from someone who knows. My experience as a Japanese-

American has taught me to be sensitive to those of other nationalities.

► Don't Assume Anything

We've learned a lot of stereotypes from our parents and the media: Blacks love watermelon; Germans are Nazis; Italians are in the Mafia. I've had people assume that I can speak Japanese fluently (I can't) or that I'm an avid sushi eater (I can't stand the stuff). Appearances can be deceiving.

► Be Careful What You Ask

Sometimes people's questions reveal that they're thinking of me as a stereotype and not a person. They may ask, "When did you come to this country?" But just because someone may look Jewish or Iranian doesn't mean he was born in Israel or Iran. America is a melting pot of all nations, and many people who look foreign were actually born here.

Or people might ask, "Do you know the Wongs, Chans or Chows?" But people who are Chinese, Japanese or of any other ethnic group don't all know each other. That seems obvious, but I've had people come up to me many times and say, "You look like Cindy Yamamoto. Do you know her?" For all the times I've been asked questions like this, I've never known the people they were talking about.

► Use Humor Carefully

Even though you're trying to be funny, people of minority races may be sensitive about jokes that remind them they're different from most people. Use slang and ethnic jokes carefully. Though I can laugh at "Ah-so" jokes, I still cringe when I hear "Jap."

But don't avoid humor entirely. It's a way of showing others that you accept them as they are, and that you're not uncomfortable talking about their uniqueness.

► Don't Call Attention to Differences

I've never had this happen, but I think I would have died if a teacher ever asked me to stand up and talk about Japan in my social studies class. I felt out of place as it was, without having people point it out even more.

Likewise, if you're in a group with someone of a different nationality or race, don't use that person as an example or an exception ("White people—oh, except Jan, of course—").

► Don't Consider Minorities Inferior

Some people seem to feel as if America and Canada are owned by whites, and that other ethnic groups are invading their territory. People with this kind of attitude forget that God is the father of all nations, and he created us all equal.

► Be Patient With People

I once dated Rick, a Caucasian. When he introduced me to his family, his father exploded. We had to break up because his family didn't approve of me. That hurt for a long time; it made me feel it was bad to be Japanese. But now I know that people like Rick's father aren't attacking me personally; somehow I threaten their security and belief systems. If you know people who are like Rick's parents and you don't agree with them, don't try to force them to change. Be patient with them. Encourage them to get to know people of other races so they'll see that underneath the face and skin-color is a human, just like them.

► Get to Know Minorities

Suppose you've tried and you still can't overcome feelings of prejudice toward certain ethnic groups. You feel it would be so much easier to just leave them alone "with their kind." Why should you even try to get to know them?

● **They can teach you a lot.** Every ethnic group has some good qualities to contribute to you and to society. Life would be awfully dull if we were all carbon copies of each other.

● **God wants people to be unified.** In the beginning, everyone spoke the same language. (See Genesis 11:1-8.) But when people began plotting to sin, God scattered them across the Earth and confused their language. Unfortunately, sin is still separating us today—sins of prejudice, hatred and bigotry. But God wants us to be unified, as

Give Happiness Away

Here are five things you can do to make others happy. Whether they're of a different race or the same as you, these ideas really work!

1. Mail a short note to a friend. The note doesn't have to be mushy. Just express gratitude for the friendship.

2. Ask a parent or a friend for advice. He or she will either faint or feel good inside . . . or both.

3. Buy someone a small gift for no particular reason. Make sure the gift doesn't coincide with Christmas or the person's birthday.

4. Take time to get acquainted with someone. Maybe you've attended school with a person for 10 years, but have never said anything to him or her. Invite yourself to sit down to eat with the person in the cafeteria and talk. Show interest in the person.

5. Make a surprise phone call. Say, "I just wanted to tell you I'm thinking about you." Be sure the person knows who you are, then hang up.

Now list two of your own ideas—things you can do to make someone happy:

1. _____
_____
_____
_____

2. _____
_____
_____
_____

he originally created us.

So the next time you see that Native American boy at the library, ask him to have a soda with you. Or talk to your African American classmate and ask her to be your lab partner. Or go jogging with your Jewish neighbor. You'll be glad you did. There's a new friend waiting for you behind the ethnic mask.

Cindy Atoji

Chapter 7
Dealing With Freddie

How Well Do You Accept Others?

Every school has its share of unique people. You know, the girl with the abundant freckles and triple-bifocal lenses. Or the guy with a pocketful of pens and the calculator hanging off his belt.

Freddie is one of those people. He's the guy many of your friends might call "weird." He has a problem making friends at school. Even at church, he's usually the brunt of all the jokes.

Many would just blame it all on Freddie. "He's just weird." "He's immature." "He has no personality." But as you read the following chapter, you may discover that Freddie isn't the problem at all.

Before you start reading, rate yourself on how you accept new and different people. Think especially about the "Freddies" in your school or youth group.

For each of the following situations, circle the way you respond most often.

1. When I see a new teenager in school, I:
   (a) say hi.
   (b) smile.
   (c) ignore him or her.

continued

2. When I'm rejected, I:
   (d) say "That's life."
   (e) seek out a good explanation for what happened.
   (f) pout.

3. No matter how hard he tries, Skeeter is a klutz. I:
   (g) avoid him.
   (h) smile at him.
   (i) say hi to him anyway.

4. My friends plan a party. I suspect they'll be drinking. I:
   (j) tell them they're evil, rotten sinners.
   (k) go to the party anyway.
   (l) tell them I can't attend because I disagree with
       their lifestyle.

5. Sherri, an honor-roll student, eats alone as if she
   doesn't want to be bothered. I:
   (m) think she's a snob.
   (n) believe she'd rather eat with someone.
   (o) say it's Sherri's right to eat alone.

6. Bob always fishes for compliments. He does crazy
   things to get attention. I:
   (p) see it as a cry for help.
   (q) realize he's acting out of insecurity.
   (r) make fun of him.

7. Someone wearing dirty overalls and long hair walks
   along the hallway as if he's lost. I:
   (s) ask if I can help.
   (t) tell my friends that he's a cave dweller looking
       for another cave.
   (u) smile, but keep walking.

8. My class-project partner is from Baghdad. I:
   (v) act like he doesn't exist.
   (w) try not to think about his differences.
   (x) wish he didn't talk funny.

9. Miss USA walks into the classroom. I:
   (y) smile shyly.
   (z) feel inferior.
   (zz) remember I have unique abilities.

continued

Your Acceptance Total

Circle the letters that correspond with your answers on the quiz. When you're through, add up the number of circles in each horizontal row. Write your total at the end of each row.

a	e	i	l	n	p	s	w	zz	Total:_____
b	d	h	k	o	q	u	x	y	Total:_____
c	f	g	j	m	r	t	v	z	Total:_____

If you received the highest score in the first row, congratulations. You're likely to accept new or different people easily.

If the second row was your top point-getter, you've done a nice job. But you can improve.

A high score in the last row shows that you need help. With some effort, you'll learn to accept new and different people.

William North

There were all kinds of reasons nobody liked Freddie Franklin. For one thing, he was sloppy. If he had either tucked in his shirt or worn it all the way out, it would have been okay. But he sort of halfway tucked it in, and it looked dumb. Besides, he wore brown socks and loafers when everybody else wore gym socks and sneakers.

Then there was the way he sat at his desk—with his shoulders kind of hunched and his head tucked down like a turtle. Or like somebody that nobody liked, which was right on the money. Nobody liked Freddie Franklin.

I guess the main reason we didn't like him was

because Jerry Chandler, president of the sophomore class and all-state fullback, didn't like him.
Jerry would wear his letter jacket to class and
look so cool. Then he'd say, "Hey, Freddie, how's
it going?" Freddie would turn pink and look
flustered and tongue-tied, and the rest of us
would laugh. Then Jerry would walk to his desk,
sit down and mimic Freddie's position—shoulders
hunched and head tucked down. We'd all giggle
or even laugh out loud. That Jerry could really
be a riot.

Knowing that nobody liked Freddie, I was in a
real bind when I got the assignment to interview
him for the school paper. I couldn't figure out
why in the world they'd want to interview him,
of all people. But it turned out that he'd won the
science fair last year; he and his father had built
a telescope in their house. I tried to get out of
the interview but couldn't.

I knew what was going to happen when the
other kids found out I had written a story about
Freddie. They'd think I thought Freddie was okay,
just because I had to do the dumb article.

Things were even worse than I had imagined
on paper day. When I walked into homeroom before the bell rang, people were already standing
around, whispering and shaking their heads. A
few glanced over at me, then quickly turned
their backs and continued their whispering.

"By Vicki Baum!" Sandra Miles sarcastically
said, not realizing I was there. "And she calls herself a reporter?"

Then she saw me. "Why don't you suggest that
the paper sponsor a 'Nerd of the Week' column,

Vicki? You could cover it. It would be right up your alley!"

Everybody laughed, and I felt my face flame. I wished I could sink through the floor. I was so humiliated that my eyes burned and I wanted to cry.

The bell was about to ring. Everyone, still smirking at Sandra's insults, started to sit down. I felt myself hunching up, trying to bury my head in my shoulders.

Then a wave went through my stomach as something hit me. How would it feel to be reject-ed and humiliated like this every single day?

"Why are you doing this to me?" I wanted to scream. "Can't you see that I'm just an ordinary person too? But your rejection is making me feel clumsy and awkward! Can't you see that you're creating your own person to laugh at, turning a normal kid into a red-faced, cringing wreck?"

And then I glanced around to see how Freddie was taking this. I was ashamed that I'd never sympathized with him before. But his seat was empty. So was Jerry's.

Next came the shock. In walked Jerry, with one arm around Freddie Franklin's shoulders! They were deep in conversation.

Was this some kind of joke? No one could de-cide whether or not to laugh.

". . . And you're sure it'll be all right with your dad?" asked Jerry, holding the school paper in his hand.

"Sure. He's always up for stargazing. Why don't you drop by around 8 o'clock?" said Freddie, his hands thrust into the pockets of his hopelessly out-of-style corduroys.

"That'll be great!" said Jerry. "Boy, I can't be-lieve I've found somebody as crazy about stars as I am! And you've even got your own telescope!"

Everyone looked at everyone else. There were a lot of puzzled looks, a couple of shrugs. I looked over at Sandra Miles, but she stared hard at her textbook. Her face registered confusion.

Freddie's shoulders looked perfectly straight for a change. I was relieved!

Jerry spent a lot of time with him after that, so everyone decided to like Freddie Franklin. Once we started, we found lots of things about him to like.

Freddie never did wear the right kind of shoes. But he acquired a reputation as the smart and absent-minded type, so everybody thought he was kind of cute. His sloppiness was now seen as an admirable disregard for the little details of life, such as tucking in shirts. Freddie, we could see, had much more important and worthwhile things on his mind. Senior year we voted him "Most Likely to Succeed."

I think of him often. I remember the way he was when we didn't like him, then the way he was when we did. The way he used to seem like a withered plant when we zapped him with our thoughtlessness, then the way he bloomed when we began accepting him for who he was. We didn't realize our own power, and we weren't aware enough of the ways we used it.

Vicki Baum Grove

Section Two

Heart to Heart: Keeping Friends

Chapter 8
Twenty-Six Ways to Say "I Like You"

How do you tell your best friend she's helped you survive the roughest day of your life? How do you let your dad know you think he's the best dad in the world? How do you gently hint that you'd like to build a deeper relationship with someone special? How do you express thanks to that teacher, pastor or youth leader who's had a major influence on your life?

Too often we hold back our affections because we're not sure how to go about it. Or we think we could never do enough to let someone know we care. Or we fear our expressions of care would be silly—or worse yet, rejected.

The uniqueness of caring is that it doesn't *have* to be expensive, wrapped in ribbons or given at special occasions. Letting someone know you care can happen in simple day-in-day-out ways.

Enjoy this encyclopedia of caring. But remember: This list is incomplete. With a bit of your own imagination and willingness to risk, you're certain to discover more than 26 ways to care!

A

Attend something that's important to that person. It might be a gymnastic meet, a family outing or worship service. Just being present is a present in itself!

B

Bake someone's favorite cookies or cake. If you're really into cooking, prepare an entire meal to accompany the dessert!

C

Create a "Care Coupon" booklet. Make up redeemable coupons such as "Good for one root beer float after school," "Free babysitting for next Saturday" or "Free hugs when needed."

D

Decorate your friend's door. Any door will do— a locker door, room door, car door or refrigerator door! Leave a clue: "I 'a-door' you!"

E

Explore a new shopping center or park together. Make it a discovery time for just the two of you.

F

Find out one thing he enjoys doing for fun. Offer to share that activity with him.

11 Ways to Lose Friends

Here are some pointers on what *not* to do if you want to keep your friends. Heed them well.

1. Never listen to your friends' point of view.

2. Rave about your accomplishments and boast about how great you are.

3. Be a fickle friend. Be insincere and dishonest in your friendships. Play games that you win at your friends' expense.

4. Don't let your friends do things the way they want to. Tell them they'd better take your advice.

5. Use your friends; get all the favors and benefits you can from them.

6. Don't help your friends or try to understand them when they come to you with their troubles. It doesn't matter how they feel or what they do; they're only friends.

7. Always make sure you have the last word in any argument or discussion.

8. Make fun of and criticize your friends every chance you get. Don't think about how you're hurting them.

9. Make all the promises you have to in order to get your friends to do things for you; then don't keep your promises.

10. Flatter your friends. Lay it on thick—especially when they don't deserve flattery or praise.

11. Always correct your friends in front of other people. Never talk to them alone about their mistakes.

B. Beck

G

Give something special. This is definitely wide-open and up to your own creative energies. Give time, support, thanks, a smile, a gift . . .

H

Hug a friend. A sure way of letting someone know she has touched your life is by giving small, medium or bone-crushing hugs.

I

Invent an "I care for you" plan. It could include a weekly talk time, a commitment to pray for that person or a friendship jar filled with tiny scrolls that tell about special times you've shared together.

J

Jot down words and phrases that express what you feel. They need not be polished—just from the heart.

K

Kidnap your friend for an early morning breakfast surprise. Or how about a group of friends for a come-as-you-are breakfast party?

L

Listen carefully to what he says. Sometimes this seems like the most difficult of all because we want to solve his problems and "make it better." Sincerely and simply listen for feelings and give your support.

M

Make a "trophy" by forming a silver person from foil, mounting it on a stand and labeling it: "Best Friend Award" or "Craziest Dancer," or whatever merits a friendship award.

N

Notice what someone is wearing or something that she accomplished. Being interested, noticing and commenting helps people feel important.

O

Order a subscription to his favorite magazine or devotional booklet as a gift.

P

Plan a surprise party in his honor. It could be on his birthday, but if there's no special occasion, it's even more of a surprise!

Q

Quote meaningful things that she's said that have been important to you—like how special it was when she told you, "I'll be there when you need me."

R

Realize and be in tune with times when someone needs a friend. Be there for them.

S

Smile a lot! Simple as it seems, a smile can kindle a spark of light on a dreary day.

T

Tell other people what your friend means to you. That's the opposite of gossip. Hearing the "good stuff" is great when it gets back to that person.

U

Understand how valuable your relationship is. Allow yourself to feel grateful for the gift of friendship God has given you.

V

Volunteer to do something for your friend. How about cleaning your friend's room or volunteering to help your friend help plan a youth retreat next month.

W

Write a note of care using the letters in your friend's name. An example could be: **C**aring **H**onest **R**isk-taking **I**nteresting **S**incere!

X

Xerox a page of your favorite friendship poems, roll it up and tie it with a ribbon. Tuck the gift in your friend's coat sleeve.

Y

Yield to your friend's needs. Being *friend-able* is being *bend-able*!

Z

Zoom to her when she needs a care-giver.

Joani Schultz

Chapter 9
When I Think I'm in Love

It was like a bad dream. There I was, 800 feet off the ground in a small airplane. I didn't know how to fly, and the guy next to me says, "Land it!"

This was not a dream! I had to gather what little flying knowledge I had and figure out how to return us safely to the ground. I concentrated on the controls and gauges. Trying to remember everything I had studied about landings, I scrutinized the approaching runway. Finally, with a bump, bounce and rumble, the plane's tires settled onto the asphalt.

"Well, that wasn't bad for your first landing," said my instructor.

My experience of learning to be a pilot taught me more than just how to fly an airplane. Odd as it sounds, I've found that flying is a lot like friendship, romance and marriage.

What I mean is that friendship and marriage are parts of a process—just like learning to fly is a process. Let me explain.

First I learned the basics of flying. Then I learned to fly a complex airplane. Then I learned to fly strictly by instruments in all kinds of weather.

I found out early that I can focus on only one part of the process at a time. Had I attempted my first landing in a complex airplane I probably would have crashed.

Friendship follows a similar process. So do love and successful marriages. If we try to take shortcuts in the process, we're in danger of crashing—and getting hurt.

► Friendship Basics

Many young people today dream of meeting someone of the opposite sex, falling in love, marrying and living happily ever after. But this rarely just happens. A solid relationship is carefully built on a firm foundation. And that foundation is friendship.

Being "just friends" with someone of the opposite sex is like learning the basics of flying. It requires a lot of work—and time. When you meet an interesting person, take time to focus on all the basic stuff. Do you both enjoy doing some of the same things? Do you have compatible senses of humor? How easily do you communicate? Do you have similar values about morals, money, family and friends? How does your faith in God and commitment to Christ compare with the other person's? Do you enjoy spending time as just friends? Would this person likely be a close friend of yours if he or she were the same sex as you?

At this beginning point in the process, try focusing your attention only on friendship. That's plenty for now. This isn't the time to focus on your friend as a romantic interest, sexual partner, marriage mate or the parent of your children. Concentrating on those things at this point short-circuits the process—and sets you up to crash.

I have a friend who loves to give flowers and candy to girls he's just met. These romantic moves usually result in a crash, because he skips the first part of the process. His leapfrogging over the simple friendship stage is like me trying to land a complex airplane in my first lesson.

The crucial friendship-building stage is often weakened when one or both people in a budding relationship are already dreaming of a house, white picket fence, three kids and a station wagon.

A good, well-worn friendship forms the roots of what may follow: romance, marriage and family.

► The Dating Stage

Once I mastered the basics of flying I was ready to move on to the next step—a more complex plane. The same is true in your relationship with someone of the opposite sex. Once your friendship has been worked on and established, then you may be ready to explore a romantic relationship.

Now is the time to check out how you relate

as male and female. How do you express feelings toward one another? Do you both feel free to share intimate thoughts and feelings with each other? Is it comfortable for each of you to talk openly about your faith in God and how that applies to your feelings toward each other? How do you show affection toward one another? Have you discussed and prayerfully reached an agreement on how far you'll go physically?

During the dating part of the process you'll want to keep practicing the basics that you worked on in the friendship stage. Keep talking; sharing your faith, values and goals; sampling a variety of activities together; and doing some things with other people.

As you move into the dating relationship, be wary of becoming preoccupied with thinking about sex or marriage or children. These concerns, dwelt on too early, have caused countless couples to crash.

Doug and Sharon had been dating a short time. They loved the thought of being married. Doug imagined himself as Ward Cleaver on *Leave It to Beaver*, returning home each day to a loving family. Sharon fantasized about how she would look on her wedding day, floating down the aisle while hundreds watched with misty eyes.

Doug and Sharon became so consumed with the wedding plans, they left no time to build a solid friendship or a mature dating relationship. The luster of *Leave It to Beaver* and wedding lace began to tarnish soon after the honeymoon.

Just because you're attracted to somebody doesn't mean you're able to live compatibly with

The Portrait of True Friendship

Any successful dating relationship has a strong friendship as its foundation. But just what are the parts that make up a true friendship?

Remember King David? Most people recognize his name. David was the greatest king Israel ever had. Far fewer, however, remember the name Jonathan. But Jonathan was one of the single greatest strengths in David's memorable life—Jonathan was his best friend.

They were from opposite backgrounds: David was a shepherd boy; Jonathan was the son of a king. Yet God gave them a rich friendship that stands out among others in the Bible.

What are some characteristics of friendship we can learn from Jonathan?

● **Love deeply.** The Bible says Jonathan loved David as much as he loved himself—and he loved him like this from the start. See 1 Samuel 18:1.

● **Be willing to sacrifice.** Jonathan at first gave his royal garments to David, then later nearly gave his life because of his loyalty to David. Friendship takes guts.

Read 1 Samuel 18:4 and 20:30-34. Is there anyone you could make that kind of commitment to? If so, who?

● **Always speak well of your friend.** More than once, Jonathan delayed his father's attempts to kill David by pointing out the good David had accomplished for Saul's kingdom. See 1 Samuel 19:4-7.

List some good things your friends have done lately:

● **Keep your promises.** Jonathan made many promises to David—promises that required risks and danger—and he kept each one. Talk about building trust! See 1 Samuel 20:12-42.

continued

Rate yourself on how well you think you keep your promises:

I never keep my promises   **I always keep my promises**

1	2	3	4	5	6	7	8	9	10

Think of three promises you have made in the last month. Write them here:

1.

2.

3.

Now really check yourself: Have some of your friends rate *you* on how well you keep promises.

● **Help your friend realize God's purpose for his or her life.** Jonathan went out of his way to encourage David in the purpose God had for him. Ever genuinely considered what God's will is for your friends—and then helped them accomplish it? See 1 Samuel 23:15-18.

List the names of your three closest friends below. Beside each name, write down one admirable quality that friend has, and a way God has used it to affect your life:

Friend #1: _____ Quality: _____

                            Effect: _____

Friend #2: _____ Quality: _____

                            Effect: _____

Friend #3: _____ Quality: _____

                            Effect: _____

Now go and tell them about it!

For more insight into true friendship, read about David and Jonathan in 1 Samuel 18—20, 23; and 2 Samuel 1.

Cindy Parolini

this person. That's why concentrating now on friendship and dating is so important—before being swallowed by endless fantasies of dancing through showers of wedding rice.

During the dating stage, work on relating as two single people.

► The Marriage Connection

After the friendship has been carefully built and the dating relationship has had time to develop, then you may wish to begin exploring the idea of marriage. Ask your pastor or other qualified counselor to help you evaluate your compatibility and preparation for married life.

Again, many couples have crashed after being distracted at this stage. For instance, if what really attracts you to marriage is the idea of having children, you've skipped an important step in the process. Focusing on children comes later.

And through it all, friendship remains the foundation. Your marriage partner should be your best friend.

This process sometimes seems like a burdensome journey. There's great temptation to jump over some of the steps. But the Apostle Paul tells us, "Love is patient."

So are you ready to fly? Be prepared to work on the relationship process one step at a time. Pray for God's Spirit to be with you as you soar together through friendship, love and marriage.

Thom Schultz

Chapter 10
When My Friends Pressure Me

Pressure Test

It's easy to feel left out when the crowd goes one way while you go another. Friends may pressure you to drink, take drugs, stay out too late or eat too much.

Guys face different pressures than girls do. But there are common pulls and pushes. Before you read this chapter, take this quiz to see how peer pressure affects—or doesn't affect—you.

1. Your friends want you to join them for some "serious shopping." You know that Gina goes gaga over designer clothes and spends big bucks. You like to wear nice clothes, but your budget requires modest purchases. You:

(a) "Borrow" your mom's credit card.

(b) Feel jealous and become angry at your dad for not raking in the bucks like Gina's father does.

(c) Have a great time at the mall, realizing Gina likes you for who you are.

2. You go to a friend's house. At the spur of the moment, someone decides to hold a seance. You've been taught not to mess with the occult. Someone teases

continued

you by saying, "I bet you're just scared your parents will find out." You:

(a) Go with the flow and try to gab with the spirits.

(b) Tell your friend to grow up.

(c) Tell your friend you wouldn't blame your parents for getting teed off. "How can I expect them to treat me like an adult if I sneak around acting like a kid?" you ask.

3. Describe one time you resisted peer pressure and felt stronger because of it. _____
_____

4. Individuals rather than groups usually influence you in positive ways. Write three names of friends who are good for you.

(a) _____
(b) _____
(c) _____

5. Many of your friends are exercise freaks. Your weight is okay, but you know you couldn't impress anyone on Muscle Beach. You:

(a) Insist only bored housewives exercise.

(b) Pull on your spandex and hop over to the Sultan of Sweat for an hour of stretching, stomping and bicep-building because everyone else does it.

(c) Hop over to the Sultan of Sweat, realizing that exercise will make you more alert, healthy and full of energy.

6. Write two ways that peer pressure has been helpful to you.

(a) _____
(b) _____

7. A group of guys sitting outside school light up a joint and ask you to smoke it. They know you're a Christian, and the jokes start. "This sure beats Sunday school." "What's the matter, Johnny? Afraid Jesus will zap you for having fun?" You:

(a) Lapse into a panic.

(b) Tell them you're a Christian and that means Christ guides what you do or don't do.

continued

(c) Mumble something about not wanting to fry your brains on drugs.

8. It's your second date and already your date is pressuring you to have sex. Your date treats you like a weirdo because you're a virgin. The pressure's on. You:

(a) Wait because God says so. You believe that God won't fail or forsake you.

(b) See how far you can get your engine revved up.

(c) Ignore the emotional, physical and spiritual consequences because being accepted is more important right now.

How did you handle these pressure pulls? You won't find clear-cut ways to stand up to the pressure. But some responses are better than others. The best way to handle these situations are: 1. (c); 2. (b); 5. (c); 7. (b); and 8. (a). How'd you rate?

William North

Welcome to the unavoidable world of peer pressure! Make no mistake, peer pressure is *pure* pressure. It causes you to behave according to group standards. It's the pressure of having your friends (peers) pushing you to do things *they* want you to do. Sometimes those things are acceptable; sometimes they're not.

How do you react when you're faced with tough decisions that put you between your friends and a hard place? Have you ever found yourself in any of these hard places?

The Conformity Club

Hard Place #1: Your parents left town for the weekend, which means you have the house to yourself. That's good!

But your parents said you can't have any friends over while they're gone. That's bad!

Two of your friends really want to party on Saturday night and with your house "available," they beg you to invite other kids over to party.

You don't think it's a wise idea, but a party would be fun! Your friends seem upset because you won't give in. Some of them are getting downright mad at you. If looks could kill, you'd be dead. *What will you do?*

Hard Place #2: Lately your friends have been wearing some outfits that you wouldn't feel comfortable wearing. They think you're strange because you won't try something new. In fact, you notice they've stopped spending as much time with you. *What will you do?*

Hard Place #3: It's Friday night and you've got a date with this great guy. Your girlfriend and her date will be going with you. You're looking forward to a great time. Well, kind of.

Your girlfriend's date does drugs and will probably pass some around. You don't want to say anything because the last time you said something, your friends really embarrassed you by their remarks. You know your girlfriend will be tempted to go along with the drugs, and you don't want to see her get involved. *What will you do?*

► Making the Right Choices

How can you make wise choices in handling negative peer pressure? The wrong way is to give in to the group, compromising your own beliefs and identity.

Here are a few suggestions that may help you find the right way:

● *Examine yourself.* Think through your values and make a list below of things you *will not do* under *any* circumstances (things such as "I will not go drinking with my friends" or "I will not use drugs"). List them now:

Things I Will Not Do Under Any Circumstances

-
-
-
-
-
-

Keep this list of personal promises handy in your room and read it often. It may be helpful for you to memorize it. Paul gave some great advice in a letter to the Romans: "Do not conform any longer to the pattern of this world, but be transformed by the renewing of your mind. Then you will be able to test and approve what God's will is—his good, pleasing and perfect will" (Romans 12:2).

● *Pray.* Ask God for the strength to keep your promises. Pray for guidance in every situation and for help to do what's right. Maybe part of your prayer can be like David's in Psalm 139:23-24.

● *Be selective in choosing close friends.* It's great to try to be a friend to everyone, but spend your time with people who have good values. You can't write on your list, "I won't use drugs," then hang out constantly with your school's biggest users. Your promise to yourself will soon crumble.

● **Be prepared.** Often your "pressure points" will come suddenly. When you feel pressured to do something you don't believe in, suggest other things the group can do. That's another list you need to make. Write down all the good things you enjoy doing with your friends and by yourself:

I enjoy this by myself	I enjoy this with my friends
●	●
●	●
●	●
●	●
●	●
●	●

Now if the crowd tries pulling you in a negative direction, suggest a different, positive activity. If the crowd votes down your alternative plans, be ready to do something on your own.

► The Flip Side

But wait! Before you tune this out as "just another peer pressure lecture," think of peer pressure this way: Peer pressure can be something to say yes to. For example, if you say no to drugs, you're actually saying yes. To what? Yourself, your health and your Christian values. If you say no to gossip, you're saying yes to showing Christian love and being a good friend.

So, yes, peer pressure *does* have a positive flip side. Here are other ways saying no means saying yes. You got that?

● *Yes to the challenge to do good.* "Anytime peer pressure motivates people to constructive actions and sensitivity to each other, it's good," says Dr. Charles Lewis, director of counseling at Wheaton College in Illinois. Peer pressure can help you get your studies done. For example, the night before a test, you and your friends can get together to learn the material. Peer pressure also motivates you to take an interest in how you look. When you hear Erica compliment Lena on her hair, you want to look good too.

You learn from your friends. Your friends can help you grow. They teach social skills such as learning how to listen and how to read body language. Friends teach you how to give and take. Peers widen your view of the world. When Jean's dad loses his job, you become fully aware of the impact of unemployment.

● *Yes to your values.* This won't always be easy, especially if you feel like you're going against everyone else. In the movie *Chariots of*

Fire, Eric Liddell refused to run the 100-meter
sprint in the 1924 Olympics because it was held
on Sunday. Although some called him a traitor to
his country, many athletes supported him. One
was so impressed by Liddell's stand that he also
followed Liddell's example at another race. By
saying no to running on Sunday, Liddell was saying yes to his faith.

It's important to establish your values and
standards *before* you feel peer pressure. Liddell's
decision wasn't a dramatic, last-minute change of
mind. Liddell and the sporting authorities had
known for a long time that he wouldn't compete
in the sprint if the heats were held on Sunday.
Liddell valued the Lord's Day more than a gold
medal. His faith was more important.

● ***Yes to taking a stand.*** When you believe
in something or make a decision, stick with it.
Of the 12 spies Moses sent to Canaan, only two,
Joshua and Caleb, believed the Israelites could
conquer the Canaanites.

Their report didn't make them celebrities. In
fact, the Israelites threatened to stone the two of
them to death. But Joshua and Caleb believed
God would go with them and not forsake them
(Numbers 13—14). And God came through.

● ***Yes to yourself.*** As you develop your
own set of moral values, you'll become more
confident. You'll become an independent and re-
sponsible decision-maker, ready to handle the
pressures you face. When you feel pressured to
do something you know is wrong, remember
that God promises to give you victory if you follow his lead.

▶ You're Not Alone

Peer pressure is nothing new. Even Jesus' peers (religious leaders) pressured him to do things their way.

Jesus had a choice: He could give in to the pressure to do and be what others demanded, or he could do what was right. Jesus, of course, chose to stand for what was right. And it cost him his life.

Likewise, if you stand by your values, you may lose a few friends. But the benefits of handling peer pressure outnumber the friends you may lose. By not crumbling to the crowd's whims and wishes, you'll find the real you and establish a true identity. You'll do things that will make you feel better about yourself. You'll also lose some false friends and find friends who will accept you for who you really are. And that's the kind of acceptance everyone wants.

Alan Maki and William North

Chapter 11
When My Friends and I Fight

Fights and Friends

Take a couple minutes and work through the following exercises. Then read the chapter to get some ideas on dealing with a friend after you've had an argument or disagreement.

Mark an X at the point on each of the following lines that best describes you.

Seems like I'm . . .

always in conflict——————————— never in conflict

Arguments are . . .

always my fault——————————— never my fault

Finding ways to solve problems with my friends are . . .

always on my mind——————————— never on my mind

Fights 'n Feelings

Think of someone you've recently had an argument with. Then complete this sentence: "After our fight, I felt . . ." Place as many answers as you can inside the pie pieces.

Get to the bottom of your feelings by writing *why* you felt the way you did. Put your answers in the appropriate circles.

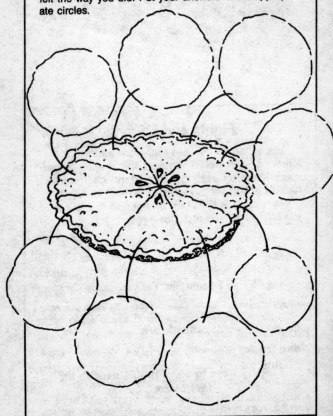

So you've had a fight with a friend. Was it one of those nasty little disagreements or a knock-down, drag-out, tooth-and-claw confrontation? What do you do now that it's over? How do you handle conflict? Or does it handle you?

My friends say don't worry about it. It'll go away. Don't get worked up about it. It's not that important. You'll get revenge later. Besides, she's not that important anyway.

She's not? You mean that same person Jesus died for?

Oh, that. Yeah, I know. Christians are weird people. (Especially her!) So now you're going to lay a religious guilt trip on me and say I've got to go make up, huh?

Well, what is your commitment as a Christian? Are you satisfied with the way things are now? Or are you willing to take a chance on God in this matter too?

All right, go ahead. I'll listen.

Okay. Let's start with the easy one. Let's suppose you blew it. (We both know how unlikely that is.) Do you realize how important tithing is to your church?

What? What does that have to do with my problem? Of course I do. I throw a little something in the pot every Sunday.

"Therefore, if you are offering your gift at the altar and there remember that your brother has something against you, leave your gift there in front of the altar. First go and be reconciled to

your brother; then come and offer your gift."
(Matthew 5:23-24).

*Hmm. That kind of looks like humility and
getting together with my brother take priority
over giving gifts to God.*

Well, can we give joyfully to God if we can't
enjoy a friend's fellowship? By the way, notice
that you are the one to go to him when you
think he has a grievance against you. Don't wait
for him to come to you.

Oh well. I don't offend people anyway.

Then let's suppose that the other person blew
it.

*Yeah, that's more like it. What does he have to
do?*

Surprise! You get to go first anyway.

What?

Yep. "If your brother sins against you, go and
show him his fault, just between the two of you.
If he listens to you, you have won your brother
over" (Matthew 18:15).

*Uh, I think I'll talk it over with my other
friend. Then I'll feel better about it.*

Nope.

*Well, can't I just tell my youth leaders about
it, and maybe something will come up in our
next meeting that will bring her around?*

Nope. Not good enough.

Then what should I do?

First, how about a thoughtful review of your
spiritual armor in Ephesians 6? It was made for
spiritual conflict and there may be some of that
in your quarrel. Give some thought especially to
that belt of truth and the gospel of peace. Then,

as they say, "Get it on!"

And pray. In particular, pray for wisdom. "If any of you lacks wisdom, he should ask God, who gives generously to all without finding fault, and it will be given to him" (James 1:5). Sort out your thoughts and take some time to consider the issues and what might be said when the two of you talk. Keep in mind that wisdom you asked for. Be gentle. Listen to her side of things.

Well. That was quite a mouthful. But this person's such a jerk. She won't pay any attention to me anyway.

Ah, but isn't the person more important than the problem?

You mean kind of like the bumper sticker: "God loves you, and I'm still trying"?

Exactly. And that's where you learn a commitment to communication. You can't know what needs you may need to meet until you understand the other person's problem.

Okay, but just suppose she won't even let me get started?

"If he will not listen, take one or two others along, so that 'every matter may be established by the testimony of two or three witnesses'" (Matthew 18:16).

Good. I can get a couple of friends and we'll stick it to her.

I don't think so. You get to find one or two of *her* friends and take them along. Don't gang up on her with a pious power play. Get people she trusts and respects, and things will go a lot smoother. She won't feel so intimidated. Besides, her friends will probably put her on the spot to get something worked out.

Yeah, good idea. But what if that really turns her off?

Then you'd better go visit with your youth leader about the third step.

That's it?

Yes, but do you see what I mean? God has equipped you not only to resolve disputes—even the world system can do that to some extent—but he has enabled you to restore relationships as well. And that's what it's all about. "So from now on we regard no one from a worldly point of view . . . Therefore, if anyone is in Christ, he is a new creation; the old has gone, the new has come! All this is from God, who reconciled us to himself through Christ and gave us the ministry of reconciliation: that God was reconciling the world to himself in Christ, not counting men's sins against them. And he has committed to us the message of reconciliation" (2 Corinthians 5:16-19). So get going!

Are you sure this is going to work?

Hey, nobody said it was going to be easy. But look at it another way. I hear some people talk about how boring school is and how dull church is. Well, God is *not* boring. If you want excitement and challenge, just follow his Word. It will keep life interesting for an eternity. Starting now.

Pete Schoon

Chapter 12
When I've Hurt a Friend

I want to tell you first of all that I'm not a bad person. I've never been in serious trouble. I do okay in school. And I'm active in my youth group at church.

But I'm a backstabber. Yeah, that's right. I'm guilty of betraying a friend's trust, of destroying a relationship and a friend's reputation.

I didn't start out this way. It just happened. And by the time I realized it, it was too late.

 November 1

I should've known something was wrong when I came out from work and saw Drew waiting for me. He knows we're not allowed to date on week nights. And besides, he should've been at basketball practice.

"I know I'm not supposed to be here," he starts before I even say hello. "But I need to talk to you for a few minutes. Can we go somewhere and sit down?"

We walk down the mall. We sit on the bench beside the shoe store.

"I hate to do this," Drew says, and my stomach tightens. "But there's no good way to break up. You see, it's changed between us, and . . ."

He drones on, but I don't hear anything past the "break up" part. I guess I should've seen it coming. But I'd hoped we could hold things together.

"And I want to still be friends," he says.

Friends. What a laugh. He dumps me and still wants to be friends.

November 15

I can hardly stand seeing Drew at school. I make a point of smiling every time I see him. I don't want him to know how hurt I am. I want him to think I'm doing just fine!

November 30

As if seeing him in school all the time isn't enough, now he's hanging around the mall with his skateboarding friends. I don't know why he's not at basketball practice, and I'm not about to ask him.

I still smile and wave when I see him, but I never feel like smiling. I wonder if he misses dating me as much as I miss him.

🐝 December 6

I see Drew and his friends around the Winter Wonderland display when I go to work. They're laughing, and he looks so happy. When he sees me, he sort of throws his head back and smiles, but I just walk past as if I don't see him.

🐝 December 8

Tonight I see some workmen dismantling Winter Wonderland. When I get to the store, I ask my manager about it.

"It was skateboarders," he says. "A bunch of 'em sneaked in after hours. Trashed the whole display—just destroyed it. They rode their skateboards all over the place, using the fake snowdrifts as ramps. The damage is irreparable."

Skateboarders? What if it was Drew? I don't have any evidence that it was him. But . . .

🐝 December 11

During prayer requests at youth group, I raise my hand. "I think we should pray for Drew, since . . . you know, since the incident at the mall with the skateboarders and all."

Murmurs start around the group. "Was that Drew?" "What a stupid thing to do." "He must be in big trouble."

I try to look concerned. I know they think I know the whole story. And really, I'm not lying. I saw Drew at the mall. And shouldn't a friend ask for prayers for another friend?

"I—I don't want to say anything more about it," I say. "Just pray for him."

 December 12

Today at school everyone talks about Drew and how much trouble they think he's in.

Drew gets called out of our fifth-hour class. My stomach tightens. In a way, I hope he's in trouble. But in another way, I hope he's innocent.

Drew's gone until a few minutes before class ends. When he comes back, he looks pale.

"Are you okay?" I ask, surprised that I feel so concerned.

"Yeah, I guess," Drew answers. "Have you heard what everyone's saying about me?"

"Uh, yeah," I stammer, not looking him in the face.

"It wasn't us!" he says. "And I don't know why anyone would think it was. Sure, we're around the mall sometimes, but we'd never do anything like that. I can't imagine who'd think we had. Someone turned our names in to mall security, and . . ."

"Is that why you got called to the office?" I ask innocently.

"Yeah," he answers. "You don't know who turned us in, do you?"

I swallow. "No, Drew. I don't know who it was."

That's the truth. I don't know who turned them in.

"Thanks anyway. I'm glad you're still my friend. I knew you'd understand."

I wish I'd been able to go to Drew and tell him what I'd done. How sorry I was, and that I'd just done it because I felt rejected and hurt that he broke up with me.

Drew trusted me, and I stabbed him in the back. What kind of a friend am I?

●

As you read the confession above, did you think of a time you "stuck it to someone" without their knowledge? Take a moment now to think about the following questions. See if they might help you discover how much of a back-stabber you may be:

● When someone hurts you, do you usually find a way to get even?

● When you do get even, do you feel satisfied?

● Do you tend to keep a mental tally of all the times someone has hurt you?

● When you hold a grudge, who do you think it really hurts more: you or the one you're mad at?

Removing the Blade

Backstabbing. It's like a fire that quickly gains momentum and burns innocent people in its path. And it's hard to stop.

How can you prevent backstabbing? Start by not playing with the matches that start it: rumors.

And check out these Bible passages. Write the fire-prevention backstabbing warnings after each verse.

"Jesus replied, ' "Love the Lord your God with all your heart and with all your soul and with all your mind." This is the greatest commandment. And the second is like it: "Love your neighbor as yourself" ' " (Matthew 22:37-39).

Warning: _____
_____
_____

"Love must be sincere. Hate what is evil, cling to what is good. Be devoted to one another in brotherly love. Honor one another above yourselves" (Romans 12:9-10).

Warning: _____
_____
_____

"Do not take revenge, my friends, but leave room for God's wrath, for it is written, 'It is mine to avenge; I will repay,' says the Lord. On the contrary: 'If your enemy is hungry, feed him; if he is thirsty, give him something to drink. In doing this, you will heap burning coals on his head.' Do not be overcome by evil, but overcome evil with good." (Romans 12:19-21).

Warning: _____
_____
_____

"Do nothing out of selfish ambition or vain conceit, but in humility consider others better than yourselves. Each of you should look not only to your own interests, but also to the interests of others" (Philippians 2:3-4).

Warning: _____
_____
_____

"Above all, love each other deeply, because love covers over a multitude of sins" (1 Peter 4:8).

Warning: _____
_____
_____

Dawn Korth

The Criticism Trap

We often fall into the trap of zapping others. Sometimes our "teasing" becomes a major way of relating. Here are two reasons why we let criticism creep into relationships.

Personal insecurity. We all feel insecure. And our own insecurity clues us in to other people's weak spots. We instinctively know how to hurt, undercut and embarrass others because we know our own insecurities.

Take Bill, for instance, who used to constantly greet his friends with remarks such as: "Have you gained weight?" "Been eating too much chocolate?" Bill was fat and unkempt in appearance. He used negative criticisms to defend against his own insecurities.

Wanting to be accepted. We all want to be accepted; we all want to "fit in." And humor often gives us a sense of community. Some youth groups may feel "Those who laugh together, stay together."

But the problem is that humor caused by negative criticism builds a phony sense of community. The reason: It's always at the expense of at least one person. Making fun of one or more group members doesn't lead to unity in the group.

As Christians, we shouldn't have to depend on the use of negative criticisms to gain personal security or to build group unity. After all, we have the greatest provision for security and unity possible—our shared life in Christ (see Ephesians 1:4).

Dennis C. Benson

Chapter 13
When White Lies Turn Dark

Lies: Good or Bad?

Before you read this chapter on lies, take a look at these results from the following surveys about white lies. How do your opinions compare with those of other kids your age? Why do you think there is a difference between your peers' opinions and those of adults?

What You Think

In a white-lies survey of teenagers, TEEN-AGE Magazine found:

- About 39 percent believe it's bad to tell white lies. Only 11 percent say it's okay.
- Ninety-seven percent admit telling white lies.
- About half say a difference exists between white lies and regular lies. Another 47 percent say there's no difference.

continued

What Adults Think

In a survey of adults, USA WEEKEND found:

- About 61 percent believe lying isn't a sin.
- Of those who think it's okay to lie, most do so to protect someone else's feelings.
- About 38 percent think other people lie to them at times.

Now, let's take a look at a real-life situation involving lying. As you read, think about how you respond to your friends' imperfections.

You're standing next to Sandra in the girls bathroom fixing your hair. Sandra, who's about 15 pounds overweight, laments, "I'm sooooooo fat!" After groping for something to say, you finally blurt out, "No, you're not."

You feel funny saying it, but then you think, Sandra isn't sooooooo fat. She's just a little overweight.

According to a TEENAGE Magazine survey, most of you agree that saying Sandra isn't fat is a white lie. But what exactly is a white lie? Webster's dictionary defines it as "a lie concerning a trivial matter, often one told to spare someone's feelings."

Is it okay to tell white lies? About 39 percent of those surveyed think telling white lies is bad.

But 48 percent say it depends on the circumstances.

The Bible never mentions white lies. And it doesn't differentiate between different kinds of lies. Leviticus 19:11 says: "Do not steal. Do not lie. Do not deceive one another." And Jesus calls Satan the "father of lies" in John 8:44.

But of course, it doesn't seem like anybody in the Bible had a friend like Sandra. What would Paul say if he knew Peter cheated on a test? What if the teacher asked Paul if Peter had cheated? Could Paul say "I don't know," if he didn't actually see Peter cheat?

If you look closely in the Bible, you can find situations where people lied. Look at Ananias and Sapphira in Acts 5:1-11. Thank goodness God's punishment for lying isn't always that severe!

Or look at Abigail in 1 Samuel 25:2-42. Abigail's husband, Nabal, got David so mad that David planned to kill all of Nabal's men. When Abigail went to David, she could've said that Nabal misunderstood why David wanted bread, water and animals. But instead, she told David the truth: Nabal was a fool. And Abigail brought David a gift to make up for Nabal's actions.

▶ Tell the Truth

God doesn't want us to tell white lies. How many times have we told a small lie only to find ourselves covering it up with a bigger one? No matter how good our intentions are, a white lie has an evil element. It has a dark side. And we can't control that evil, dark side.

Think about Sandra. You won't help solve her weight problem by telling her a white lie. And your lie can break down the trust between you.

So instead of "white lying" in response to Sandra's comment, you can:

● **Listen.** Help Sandra explore her feelings. If you say, "Sounds like you're frustrated about your weight," you give her a chance to say more about what she's feeling.

● *Give alternatives.* Instead of agreeing or disagreeing, help Sandra explore alternatives. Say, "If you want to lose weight, try our exercise class at church."

● *Tell the whole truth.* You may need to do more than agree or disagree. Disagreeing won't help Sandra and neither will agreeing. If you were once overweight, explain how you understand her problem. Show your support.

► Think on Your Feet

Unfortunately, it's hard to think of alternatives when you need them. But you can learn to think on your feet. Try these ways to improve your "truth skills."

● *Take your time.* Don't jump in with your first thought. If you think about what you want to say, your thoughtfulness will show. And Sandra will wait for your response.

● *Think about Sandra's situation.* Why is Sandra complaining about her weight? Find out how she's feeling. Ask questions.

● *Think about Jesus.* What would Jesus do in your position? Thinking of what Jesus would do may help you find the most loving, truthful response.

● *Pray.* You've taken time to think of a response, but you still feel uncomfortable. Before saying anything, ask for God's help. Then trust that he'll watch over your situation. Feel confident that you're giving the best response available, even if it's a simple yes.

● *Think again.* Sometimes you blow it. You realize you could've been more truthful. Review the situation. What other responses could you have given? Learn from your mistakes.

● *If you lie, apologize.* Instead of looking for justification, ask for forgiveness. In TEENAGE Magazine's survey, one person said, "God doesn't like white lies, but he understands them."

That's true of all our sins. God knows why we do what we do. We may think some justifications are better than others. But these justifications don't erase sin. Only God's forgiveness can do that.

Karen J. Fisher

Wiping Out White Lies

If 97 percent of teenagers admit to telling a white lie now and then, it may be difficult to reverse the trend. Using suggestions from the article, how would you respond to these situations?

Situation One: Your friend asks you to cover for him on Saturday night. He told his parents he's staying at your house, but he's actually going camping with his girlfriend. That Saturday night, his parents call to talk to him.

You're tempted to say:

If Jesus were in this predicament, he'd say:

You pray:

And now you say:

Situation Two: Your big math assignment is due today. But you put it off and never did it. Your teacher asks you what happened.

You're tempted to say:

If Jesus were in this predicament, he'd say:

You pray:

And now you say:

Chapter 14

When I Hate Someone

Have you ever really hated someone? And then wondered if you could still be a Christian while hatred brewed inside you?

"I hate her," Lisa said to our Bible class. "I hate Shelly so much I could kill her, and I think I would if I had the chance."

Lisa usually doesn't talk this way. She's a friendly girl who's active in church. So how could a Christian have so much hatred?

Someone asked her what happened. Lisa explained that she'd ratted on Shelly who broke the law. Then Shelly's friends came after Lisa. "We had it out," Lisa said. "I got pushed around a lot. So much hatred just built up inside me."

▶ Everyone Hates

Hatred is a common experience. And being a Christian doesn't mean you never hate. We all have to deal with hatred in ourselves—and others.

In 1 John 4:20, John says you can't love God if you hate your brother. And the next verse has a tough-to-obey command: "Whoever loves God must also love his brother."

But Christians hate. How do we square that with John's words? Are most Christians phonies and not Christians at all, or do most Christians hate sometimes?

Even when Christians sin, they live in God's grace. We are God's children. And grace means that we are accepted for who we *are*, rather than what we *do*. Sin is an abomination to God. But no sin is big enough to shut off God's unimaginable grace. So it's possible to hate and still have God's unmerited love for us. There's a lot of comfort in that.

► Hatred Separates

But hatred can also drive a wedge between you and God. If you decide that someone has done something that you can't forgive, then you'll stop caring for that person. And if you stop caring about him or her and wish that person only harm, how can you believe God—or anyone—will forgive and love you (Matthew 6:14-15)?

Hatred separates. You don't want to be near a person you hate. You may have heard that we meet God in every person. If we pick out one person we don't want to be around we also say we don't want to be around God. John says it simply, "We can't say we love God and hate our brother."

There are many ways we can hate our brother. Our Bible class agreed that there is "puppy hate" just like there is "puppy love." Puppy hate can be serious, but isn't real hate. It doesn't last long and you don't stop caring about the person while you're experiencing it.

► Hardcore Hatred

But you can hate someone more than at a puppy-hate level. In our class, Tim said this higher hatred level is when "you can't stand a person at any time or under any circumstance." This kind of hatred lasts a long time, but doesn't have to last forever.

This longevity is one reason hatred differs from anger. Anger is a feeling. It comes over you suddenly and quickly disappears. And you can be angry with someone you love.

But hatred is different; it's a decision instead of a feeling. You choose not to love and not to care about a person. That makes hatred serious business. It's the opposite of love. And love not only makes the world go around, but is the keystone of Christian living.

► The First Step

If you're honest, there will be times when you say you hate somebody. Lisa said it in our Bible class. Talking about hatred is an important step. It's called confession when you admit your hatred and don't want to continue hating.

But talking about hatred won't get rid of it. After you admit it, you must try to get over it. And the only way to rid yourself of hatred is to replace it with love.

Going directly from hatred to love is too big a step for most of us. I'm sure it would be for Lisa. But you can start by asking for God's help to become concerned and wish the best for the person you hate.

In that way you move from hatred toward love. And it helps to know that God loves you even when you hate.

If love makes the world go around, then hatred stops it. We want to move from hatred to love. So now is the time to start moving.

Eldor Kaiser

Your Hatred Thermometer

When someone hurts you, it's easy to hate that person. Read the following situations. In the space after each situation, indicate the level of hatred you'd feel by writing a number from 1 (for a mild, puppy hate you think would pass in a few days) to 10 (for a hate so strong you'd never talk to that person again).

A friend tells you you're fat.

A stranger steals your 10-speed bike.

Your father grounds you for a month.

A police officer gives you a speeding ticket, and your insurance rates double.

Your sister slaps you for borrowing her records.

A drunk driver crashes into your dad and kills him.

Your best buddy asks your steady girlfriend for a date, and she breaks up with you.

Your mother doesn't care that you won a state solo music competition.

The first-string quarterback doesn't invite you to his party.

Your brother gets better grades than you do.

What's Your Temperature?

When you finish, add up all the numbers in the blanks. If you scored 10 to 30, congratulations. You have a low temperature and know how to handle hatred well. If you scored 31 to 60, it's easy for you to hate, and you need to get to know people and learn their good qualities. If you scored 61 to 100, you have a high hatred fever. Begin confessing your hatred and turning it into love.

Afraid to let them know

Chapter 15
When My Friend's Not a Christian

● Marsha's face flushed as she tried to find the right words to explain why she couldn't attend the party. Heather was just beginning to become a close friend and Marsha didn't want to jeopardize that relationship. Yet she knew that this party's highlight would be drinking—maybe drugs too. And as a Christian, she didn't feel comfortable with that.

● Why was Phil's heart beating so? He'd been sitting in the cafeteria with three friends. Suddenly the subject changed to religion. One of his friends said that religion was for weak people and that God was a figment of man's imagination. Another simply said that God was weird. Phil, a Christian, kept quiet, but when he left the cafeteria he carried with him a lot of unidentified emotions and a good measure of guilt.

Both Marsha and Phil faced problems that many Christian young people face every day. It *is* hard to live the Christian life among non-Christian friends. But while there aren't pat answers to make it easy, some guidelines can help.

First, let's look at the problem. Here are three possible reactions that Christians can have when they're around non-Christian friends. Which best describes the way you respond?

▶ Three Possible Reactions

● **Develop a pious, self-righteous attitude.** This choice solves many problems because it builds a cocoon of "safety." These Christians alienate themselves from non-Christians and mainly associate with people who are like themselves.

This approach, however, runs contrary to the example Christ set, and it negates his command for Christians to be the salt of the earth. Christ himself was criticized for hanging around with the "wrong" kind of people. He responded, "It is not the healthy who need a doctor, but the sick" (Matthew 9:12).

People who aren't Christians desperately need to see a Christian example in their world. But if Christianity is lived only within the safety of church walls and tight circles of like-minded friends, how can it have the life-changing effect that Jesus intended it to have?

● **Blend in and not make waves.** These Christians become chameleons for Christ—

members of God's secret service. Their lives and words are no different from those of non-Christians around them. This option, therefore, also offers almost total freedom from the hassles of explaining the Christian faith or resolving problems that arise from a different lifestyle.

The difficulty with this approach is that it compromises Christianity; Jesus said that Christians should not be able to blend in with the world. (See John 17:14-16.) The outer conflicts of being Christians are eliminated, but the price these Christians pay is an inner conflict that is a hundred times more stressful. They know their compromises aren't making God very happy.

● **Take a Christian stand among non-Christian friends.** Unlike the first two responses, this one doesn't even hint at being the easiest. It's not. But for sincere Christians, it's the most honest and challenging lifestyle.

► How to Be a Christian Among Non-Christian Friends

Here are six tips to help:

● **Be serious about being a Christian.** The most successful people in any field are those who are totally committed to what they believe. Are you sure you want to be a Christian—to live a life like Jesus'? If so, keeping that goal in mind will help keep you on track when you're with your friends. If you're not serious about being a Christian, confusion and guilt will reign because you're not sure what you want.

● **Set personal standards.** And know why

you've chosen them. Marsha might have answered Heather's invitation with "It's against my religion" or "My parents won't let me." Either answer, however, suggests that she's under unwanted restriction. If Marsha had set her own standards and really believed and understood them, then a sensible answer would be "I'd really rather not" or "I've decided not to go to parties where alcohol is served." She may then be asked why. This question would open the door for a personal, simple explanation of her faith and why she's set standards in her own life.

● **Be considerate of others' feelings.** Sadly, it's easy to come off with a "holier than thou" attitude. One of the reasons Phil may have been so upset was that he felt the need to convince his friends that his beliefs were right—and theirs were wrong. But successful sharing of faith doesn't mean winning arguments about God. Sometimes careful listening and stimulating questions are the best ways to invite friends to be interested in Christianity.

● **Be vulnerable.** When you make a mistake, admit it. The ability to say "I'm sorry, I was wrong" goes a long way toward helping your friends see that Christianity is for real people. When you feel you've said or done something inappropriate for a Christian, tell your close friends you feel bad about it. Then start again, trying your best to live as a Christian.

● **Know the cost.** If you take a stand for anything, it will cost you some friends. But if a friend deserts you because of your faith, you didn't have much of a friend in the first place. It

Inviting a Friend to Youth Group

Have you ever wondered how other kids seem to always bring visitors to youth group when you can't even get your best friend to attend with you?

Well, here are some proven tips that can help you overcome "invitation phobia," and ease the way for you to ask a friend to church:

● **Show genuine interest in the person you're asking.** Get to know the person. If you're asking a friend from school, eat lunch together, talk between classes or stay after school to get to know him or her better.

● **Be willing to spend time with them on their turf.** This doesn't mean you should compromise your values when spending time with a friend. But, if he or she is involved in art or sports, be willing to go along to an art gallery or a tournament. Meeting friends halfway will make them more open to going someplace new with you.

● **Bring your visitor with you.** Giving people a ride lets them know you don't mind going out of your way for them and you really care. And people are less likely to change their minds about attending if someone's picking them up.

● **Introduce your guest.** Tell everyone something about your friend. This may bring up a topic or activity someone else will discuss with your visitor.

● **Stay with the person you invite.** Nothing is more uncomfortable than being left alone in a room full of strangers.

● **Stay in tune with your friend's feelings and body language during the meeting.** Is he or she open to what's being discussed? If so, after the meeting may be the perfect time to share about your relationship with Christ.

● **Don't be discouraged if you're turned down.** Maybe the person you asked has had a bad experience with "religion," or his or her family has never made church a priority. Be open and understanding and, most of all, still be a friend.

So why not invest some of your time in another person? Go ahead; extend an invitation that could change a life.

Teresa Cleary

works in reverse too. If you decide to ignore a person because he or she doesn't believe as you do, you are not much of a friend either.

● **Have a support group of Christian friends.** All of the above information is not meant to suggest that Christians should have no Christian friends. On the contrary, a group of supportive believers is invaluable. All Christians need Christian friends who will confront and help on a regular basis.

●

So remember: If you know what you believe and are committed to living those beliefs among your friends, you will have a challenging, exciting life. Learn to relax and be comfortable with your faith and the standards you've set for yourself. If you're not nervous and uncomfortable about being a Christian, your friends won't be bothered about it either.

One more tip: Instead of worrying about how many people will be your friends because you're a Christian, focus on how many people you, as a Christian, can befriend.

And keep in mind that you're not alone. Thousands of Christians successfully live their faith among non-Christians every day. And the God of the universe, your greatest friend, is with you every step of the way.

Ken Davis